Garlic

About Garlic

A Spice with Tradition

In countries where people reach an incredible age, garlic has always played a large role in the kitchen. Originally, garlic came from the wide steppe regions of Southeast Asia, and then, via China, India, and the Near East, it reached Southern Europe, where the Romans gave it the botanic name *Allium*, which is still used today. In the entire Mediterranean region, cooks value garlic as an indispensable spice for meat, fish, and vegetable dishes, to which it gives a unique, and fabulous, intense flavor.

Tips and Tricks

In Europe, the main regions where garlic is grown are in Italy, Spain, and Southern France. In these regions, at harvest time, the ripe garlic heads are pulled up, along with the wilted leaves, which can then be braided into artful braids and bundles. This looks fun, and it makes a tempting decoration in a home. One should however not keep it for too long as just a delight for the eyes: Garlic left too long to dry will eventually and naturally fall apart and turn into garlic powder. Remember, freshly harvested garlic is the most flavorful. That way it also has the advantage of not leaving penetrating and lasting scent traces—thus one can use it generously! Garlic eaters among themselves are not bothered by a light scent anyway. And for very sensitive people, there are a few proven tips: Eat a lot of fresh parsley (or other green herbs with a high content in chlorophyll), which has always been recommended as a breath freshener. One can also chew a few coriander seeds, as done in the Near East. Or drink plenty of milk, or red wine—all this helps!

To remove garlic scent from your hands: Rub them thoroughly with lemon or salt, then rinse with cold water. Afterwards use a good lotion—it makes the hands soft and smooth.

The Healing Powers of Garlic

They are no longer disputed even by the most serious scientists: It is certain that garlic has a strong antibiotic, i.e. an inhibiting effect on harmful bacteria, that it can lower blood pressure as well, and that it aids digestion, and helps prevent hardening of the arteries. These beneficial powers are best realized when you use the fresh, whole garlic. Garlic pills, as much as they are praised, are of such varying quality, that they are not always a fully adequate replacement. But there are even more benefits in garlic: Though today no one seriously believes any longer that it helps in driving away vampires and evil spirits, it is being rediscovered as a completely natural means of pest control. A few cloves have worked wonders, when planted in the earth next to roses, or among other potted plants, which are infested with aphids. And when, after some time, fresh garlic green is sprouting, use it like chives as an herb.

Purchasing Garlic

It is best to buy garlic where you get your fresh vegetables: at the farmers' market, or at a market with an impeccably run produce department. And buy only as much garlic as you will use within a week. Make sure the garlic is firm and juicy, that the peel shines silken, that the spot where the stem is cut is neither dried out nor wilted. (This is the spot for recognizing fresh garlic—dried out garlic usually has a shriveled up stem end.) Whether you buy white garlic, or the popular pink one, is not so important—perhaps the pink one tastes a touch milder. A third kind, elephant garlic, boasts huge cloves and a mild flavor.

Storing Garlic

Store garlic in a dry, airy place where it's not too warm. Ideally, it should be kept in a small basket in a cool, dark place. In the refrigerator it loses much of its flavor.

Preparing Garlic

First peel the garlic head, then separate the cloves, and remove the fine skin from them, if you want to use the whole clove. If you press them through a garlic press, you can leave the fine skins on, as they remain in the press. It is easier to peel the garlic if you blanch it briefly, that is, put them into boiling water. But only do this for a few seconds; otherwise the cloves will lose their flavor. This method is of interest particularly for recipes that require a lot of garlic; otherwise plan on a lot of time for peeling. You can also soak them for half an hour in cold water, or heat them in a microwave oven very briefly. Should you find a small green center when you cut the garlic (a sign that it is no longer quite fresh), cut it out, as it can taste bitter. The spiciest and most intense flavor is from finely chopped, raw garlic. Incidentally, you can also smash the cloves with a wide, heavy knife blade on a chopping board, the way professional cooks do—it saves a lot of time! Garlic that is pressed through a press tastes a little subtler, as part of the clove is left behind. The flavor becomes even milder if you cook or sauté it along with the food. Be careful not to add it to hot oil, as it burns quickly and then tastes bitter. If you want only a touch of garlic flavor, add the whole, unpeeled cloves to the dish you are cooking or sautéing, and remove them before serving.

Garlic-Almond Soup

A specialty from sunny Andalusia.

Serves 4:
8 cloves garlic
2 tbs butter
5 oz peeled, ground
   almonds
4 1/4 cups chicken stock
8 red grapes (optional)
Salt to taste
Freshly ground white
   pepper to taste
1 pinch freshly grated
   nutmeg
2 tbs fresh lemon juice
1/2 bunch fresh thyme

Prep time: about 50 minutes
Per serving: 310 calories
9 g protein/ 27 g fat
7 g carbohydrates

1 Peel the garlic cloves and cut crosswise into fine slices.

2 Heat the butter in a pot, and fry the garlic until golden brown over low heat. Add the almonds and roast them briefly. Add the chicken stock, bring to a boil, and simmer gently, covered, for 25 minutes.

3 Meanwhile wash the grapes, halve them, and remove any seeds.

4 Season the soup with salt and pepper, the nutmeg, and the lemon juice.

5 Serve the soup in bowls and add the grapes. Wash the thyme, pull off the leaves, and garnish the soup with them.

Garlic-Cream Soup with Cheese Toasts

For a more filling soup, use 2 slices of bread and a little more cheese per cup.

Serves 4:
1 medium onion
2 tbs butter
12 cloves garlic
2 tbs flour
3–3 1/4 cups beef stock
1 cup heavy cream
4 slices baguette, about
   1/2-inch thick
Salt to taste
Freshly ground black
   pepper to taste
1 pinch freshly grated
   nutmeg
1 tbs fresh lemon juice
2 tbs freshly grated
   Appenzeller or
   Emmentaler
   cheese
1 tsp dried oregano

Prep time: about 45 minutes
Per serving: 430 calories
5 g protein/35 g fat
14 g carbohydrates

1 Peel the onion and chop it finely. Heat the butter in a pot, and sauté the onion until it is translucent. Peel the garlic, cut the cloves in quarters lengthwise, and briefly sauté with the onion.

2 Stir in the flour until golden. Stir in the beef stock and the heavy cream and simmer, covered, over medium heat, for about 20 minutes.

3 Preheat the oven to 475° F, or preheat the broiler.

4 Toast the baguette slices.

5 Puree the soup well with a regular blender or hand blender, season with salt, pepper, nutmeg, and the lemon juice, and pour it through a strainer into four bowls. Place the bread on top, sprinkle with the cheese, and bake in the oven (middle rack), or under the broiler, until golden brown. Before serving, sprinkle with a little oregano.

Above: Garlic-Almond Soup
Below: Garlic-Cream Soup
with Cheese Toasts

Puree of Red Lentil Soup

Red lentils are available in natural foods stores, specialty foods shops, and Asian markets.

Serves 4:
1 medium-sized leek
2 tbs butter
4 cloves garlic
1/2 cup dry white wine
8 oz dried red lentils
4 1/4 cups vegetable stock
Salt to taste
Freshly ground black
  pepper to taste
A pinch of cayenne pepper
1 tbs fresh lemon juice
1/2 cup sour cream
A few leaves of fresh
  chervil for garnish

Prep time: about 45 minutes
Per serving about: 860 calories
14 g protein/73 g fat
30 g carbohydrates

1 Trim the leek, slit open lengthwise, wash thoroughly, and slice the white and light green parts into thin strips.

2 Heat the butter in a pot, and steam the leek rings briefly.

3 Peel the garlic cloves, mince, and add to the leek rings.

4 Slowly mix in the white wine, stirring constantly; bring to a brief boil.

5 Add the lentils and the vegetable stock. Heat to boiling, then simmer at very low heat for about 20 minutes, until the lentils are completely soft. Season with salt, black pepper, and cayenne pepper.

6 Puree the soup with a regular blender or hand blender; push it through a sieve, and bring to a brief boil once more. Add the lemon juice, and check the seasonings again.

7 Pour the soup into four soup plates or bowls, and put a dollop of sour cream and a few chervil leaves on each serving.

Originating in Asia, lentils came from Egypt to the Romans, and thus also to the rest of Europe. Red lentils do not need to soak, and are done in a surprisingly short amount of time. From India and Turkey they come to the market already peeled. Their flavor is very mild, and is nicely complemented by spices such as garlic. By the way, they change their color during the cooking process, and turn a strong yellow.

Puree of Red Lentil Soup

Romesco

This very garlicky, Spanish-style sauce is delicious, warm or cold, with steamed or fried fish, meat, eggs, or as a fondue dipping sauce.

Serves 4:
1 large tomato
1 red bell pepper
1/2 cup olive oil
6 cloves garlic
2 tbs ground almonds
1 tbs bread crumbs
Salt to taste
Freshly ground black
  pepper to taste
A dash of hot paprika
1/2 bunch fresh Italian
  parsley

Prep time: about 40 minutes
Per serving: 330 calories
3 g protein/34 g fat
7 g carbohydrates

1 Briefly plunge the tomato into boiling water, remove the skin, and chop the flesh finely, removing the stem and seeds. Wash the bell pepper, remove the seeds and thick ribs, and dice very finely.

2 Heat the olive oil in a pot. Briefly sauté the bell pepper and tomato. Peel the garlic, press, and add to the pot. Sauté everything, over medium heat, for about 20 minutes, until all ingredients are well combined.

3 Puree the vegetables with the almonds and the bread crumbs in a blender. Season to taste with salt, pepper, and paprika.

4 Wash the parsley, shake dry, chop finely, and mix it in.

Garlic Puree

Makes a nice sauce for lamb or fish.

Serves 4:
3 heads of garlic
2 tbs butter
Salt to taste
Freshly ground black
  pepper to taste
1 tsp fresh thyme leaves
  (or 1/2 tsp dried)

Prep time: about 30 minutes
Per serving: 120 calories
3 g protein/6 g fat
14 g carbohydrates

1 Separate the garlic heads into cloves, peel these, and place them in a pot. Add cold water to cover them. Slowly heat to boiling, reduce the heat, and simmer for about 3 minutes.

2 Pour off the water, again cover the garlic cloves with cold water, and bring to boiling. Repeat this procedure five times.

3 Pour off the water, puree the garlic with the butter in a blender, and season the puree with salt, pepper, and the thyme. Store in a cool place.

Garlic Butter

Serves 4:
4 oz soft butter
6 cloves garlic
Salt to taste
Freshly ground white
  pepper to taste
1 tsp fresh lemon juice

Prep time: about 8 minutes
Per serving: 240 calories
1 g protein/26 g fat
2 g carbohydrates

1 Place the butter in a small bowl. Peel the garlic, mince, and add to the butter. Season with the salt and pepper, and add the lemon juice.

2 Mix the ingredients thoroughly with a fork, and refrigerate.

Pesto Genovese

Pesto is an herb past from Genoa, Italy. It is best made with fresh basil. Also important is the quality of olive oil. Cold pressed, unrefined, extra-virgin olive oil is the best. Pesto tastes good with pasta, but also with cooked meat, fish, or poultry. With a spoonful of pesto, a simple salad dressing is enhanced with a Mediterranean flavor. You can prepare pesto ahead of time. Covered with olive oil in little jars with screw-on lids, it keeps for six weeks in the refrigerator.

Serves 6:
3–4 bunches fresh basil
1/2 tsp salt
4 cloves garlic
2 tbs pine nuts
1/2 cup extra-virgin olive oil
3 oz Parmesan cheese, freshly grated
Freshly ground black pepper to taste

Prep time: about 15 minutes
Per serving: 290 calories
6 g protein/27 g fat
2 g carbohydrates

1 Rinse off the basil, shake dry, pick the leaves from the stems, and chop the leaves finely.

2 Place them in a bowl and sprinkle the salt over them. Peel the garlic, press, and add to the bowl.

3 With a food processor, grind the pine nuts finely, and add to the bowl.

4 Slowly stir in the olive oil, until a thick paste is obtained. At the end, stir in the Parmesan cheese, one spoonful at a time. Season the pesto with pepper.

> **Tip!** For the best texture, chop everything by hand, or use a mortar and pestle. Alternatively, you can pulse all of the ingredients together in a food processor until the desired texture is reached.

Roasted Eggplant Spread with Sheep's Cheese

Eggplant caviar is another name for this hearty spread. In Turkey and Greece it is served along with other hors d'oeuvres.
It is also delicious as a spread for bread, with broiled fish, or especially delicious with fresh potatoes boiled with their skins.

Serves 4:
2 eggplants (each about 10 oz)
3 tbs olive oil
4 cloves garlic
9 oz sheep's-milk feta cheese
1 tbs fresh lemon juice
Salt to taste
Freshly ground black pepper to taste
1 tsp fresh oregano (or 1/2 tsp dried)

Prep time: about 1 hour and 10 minutes
Per serving: 260 calories
11 g protein/20 g fat
7 g carbohydrates

1 Heat the oven to 425° F. Wash the eggplants and cut them in half lengthwise. Brush the cut sides with the olive oil.

2 Place aluminum foil, shiny side up, on a baking sheet. Place the eggplants on it, cut side down. Place in the oven, (middle rack), and bake about 30 minutes.

3 Take the eggplant out and remove the stems. Peel the garlic, and puree it with the eggplant and the sheep's-milk cheese in a blender.

4 Season the eggplant puree with the lemon juice, salt, pepper, and the oregano, and let cool for about 30 minutes.

Tzatziki

Cucumber-Yogurt Sauce with Garlic

Serves 4:
1 cucumber
16 oz plain yogurt
4 cloves garlic
1 tbs olive oil
Salt to taste
Freshly ground black
  pepper to taste
1/2 bunch fresh dill

Prep time: about 15 minutes
Per serving: 120 calories
5 g protein/7 g fat
9 g carbohydrates

1 Peel the cucumber, cut in half lengthwise, and scrape out the seeds with a spoon. On a box grater, grate the cucumber over the large holes, and press it dry in a kitchen towel.

2 Put the yogurt in a bowl and stir smooth.

3 Peel the garlic, mince, and add to the bowl. Add the oil, salt, pepper, and mix in the grated cucumber.

4 Rinse the dill, shake dry, pick it off the stems, chop finely, and mix in. Refrigerate the Ttzatziki until serving; season to taste with salt and pepper.

Aïoli

From Provence, aïoli works as a dip, fondue dipping sauce, or accompaniment to vegetables, fish, and meat dishes.

Serves 4:
4 cloves garlic
2 very fresh eggs
Salt to taste
Freshly ground black
  pepper to taste
1/2 tsp Dijon-style
  mustard
1 cup extra-virgin olive oil
3 tbs fresh lemon juice

Prep time: about 10 minutes
Per serving: 600 calories
2 g protein/65 g fat
2 g carbohydrates

1 Peel the garlic cloves, and mince, and place in a mixing bowl.

2 With a thumbtack, carefully prick a hole in the eggs. Place the eggs in a pot of boiling water for 60 seconds and remove. Crack open the eggs, separating the yolks from the whites. Discard the whites. Add the egg yolks to the bowl with the garlic and stir, seasoning with salt and pepper.

3 Add the mustard and very slowly pour the olive oil in a thin stream, constantly beating it with a hand mixer, until a mayonnaise consistency is obtained.

4 Season the aïoli with the lemon juice and pepper.

Garlic Sauce with Walnuts

Specialty from Cyprus

Serves 4:
2 day-old white rolls
6 cloves garlic
1/4 cup olive oil
2 tbs white wine vinegar
Salt to taste
Freshly ground black
  pepper to taste
1/2 bunch fresh Italian
  parsley
2 tbs chopped walnuts
6 black olives

Prep time: about 30 minutes
Per serving: 170 calories
3 g protein/15 g fat
8 g carbohydrates

1 Soak the rolls in water for 15–20 minutes.

2 Peel the garlic cloves, and press them into a bowl through a garlic press.

3 Press the rolls dry, and add them, along with the oil and the vinegar, to the garlic. Mix well, and season with salt and pepper.

4 Rinse the parsley, pick it from the stems, and chop medium finely. Mix it, along with the walnuts, into the sauce.

5 Place the sauce in a bowl, and garnish with the olives. Refrigerate the Ttzatziki until serving.

Hor D'Oeuvres, Snacks, and Side Dishes

What Else You Can Do with Garlic?

How about trying a trick of Southern French cuisine: Bake whole, peeled cloves of garlic, wrapped in foil, along with a roast (for instance, leg of lamb), until they are soft as butter. That way the cloves taste much milder, and can be spread on bread like butter — delicious as hors d'oeuvres with an aperitif, or as a side dish to the meat. The garlic puree can also be used as a filling for little puff pastry shells or mini cream puffs. Or you can mix it with cream, a little salt and pepper, and you have an elegant sauce or dressing.

Garlic Bread

Serves 4:
6 oz soft butter
6 cloves garlic
1/2 bunch fresh Italian
  parsley
Salt to taste
Freshly ground white
  pepper to taste
A pinch of cayenne pepper
1 baguette

Prep time: about 30 minutes
Per serving: 600 calories
11 g protein/33 g fat
63 carbohydrates

1 Put the butter in a bowl. Peel the garlic, mince, and add to the bowl.

2 Rinse the parsley, pick the leaves from the stems, chop the leaves very finely, and add to the bowl. Season the butter with the salt, white pepper, and cayenne pepper, mix well, and refrigerate.

3 Preheat the oven to 400° F.

4 Slice the baguette three-quarters of the way through, making 3/4-inch-thick slices, and place a dab of the garlic butter into each of the slits.

5 Wrap the bread in aluminum foil, and bake in the oven (middle rack) for about 15 minutes. It is best served warm.

Bruschetta

Garlic Bread, Italian-Style

Serves 4:
4 cloves garlic
8 slices country-style white
  bread, about 1/2-inch
  thick
1/2 cup extra-virgin olive
  oil
Salt to taste
Freshly ground black
  pepper to taste

Prep time: about 15 minutes
Per serving: 260 calories
4 g protein/17 g fat
25 g carbohydrates

1 Peel the garlic cloves, and cut in half lengthwise.

2 Toast the bread golden brown, and while still warm, rub thoroughly with the cut sides of the garlic.

3 Drizzle the oil over them, season with salt and pepper, and eat immediately.

Tomato Bruschetta

Specialty from Spain

Serves 4:
1 ripe large tomato
3 tsp extra-virgin olive
  oil
Salt to taste
Freshly ground black
  pepper to taste
4 cloves garlic
8 slices baguette, about
  1/2-inch thick

Prep time: about 25 minutes
Per serving: 170 calories
5 g protein/5 g fat
27 g carbohydrates

1 Briefly plunge the tomato into boiling water, remove the skin and seeds, and chop the flesh finely. Mix with the olive oil, salt, and pepper.

2 Peel the garlic cloves, and cut in half lengthwise.

3 Toast the bread, and rub with the cut side of the garlic cloves.

4 Spread the tomato mixture on the slices of bread. Serve at once.

Garlic Bread (left), Bruschetta (middle, right), and Tomato Bruschetta (back).

Garlic Bread with Two Kinds of Cheese

A tasty snack or tidbit paired with wine or beer.

Serves 4:
1 long baguette
8 cloves garlic
6 oz mozzarella cheese
2 tbs freshly grated Emmentaler cheese
1 bunch fresh Italian parsley
2 tbs soft butter
1/2 tsp salt
A pinch of Freshly ground black pepper
Freshly grated nutmeg to taste

Prep time: about 30 minutes
Per serving: 480 calories
20 g protein/15 g fat
63 g carbohydrates

1 Slit the baguette open on the side, and pull out some of the bread to make a pocket for the filling.

2 Peel the garlic cloves, and mince, and add to a bowl. First, slice the mozzarella, then dice it, and, along with the Emmentaler, put it in the bowl.

3 Wash the parsley, shake it dry, chop finely, and, along with the butter, add it to the cheese. Mix everything well, and season with the salt, pepper, and nutmeg. Preheat the oven to 400° F. Fill the split-open baguette with the cheese mixture, and cut diagonal slices, about 1-inch thick, three quarters of the way through the bread.

4 Place the bread on a foil-lined baking sheet, and bake in the oven (middle rack) for about 10 minutes. Serve it hot, straight from the oven.

Tip! You can prepare the bread ahead of time. Wrap it in aluminum foil and keep it in the refrigerator until you're ready to put it in the oven.

Cream Cheese Spread with Bacon and Zucchini

This hearty spread tastes terrific spread on dark bread or as a dip for crisp vegetables.

Makes about 4 cups:
2 zucchini
8 cloves garlic
10 oz bacon
16 oz cream cheese, softened
Salt to taste
Cayenne pepper to taste
Lemon juice to taste

Prep time: about 30 minutes
Per serving: 413 calories
16 g protein/37 g fat
4 g carbohydrates

1 Rinse the zucchini and cut into small dice. Peel the garlic and slice finely or mince.

2 Dice the bacon into small pieces and cook in a skillet until very crisp. Add the zucchini and garlic to the skillet and sauté briefly. Strain the bacon-vegetable mixture through a strainer.

3 Put the cream cheese in a bowl and stir until smooth. Add the bacon-vegetable mixture and mix well.

4 Season the mixture with salt, a dash of cayenne pepper, and lemon juice.

Tip! Very simple and always good: Rub freshly roasted bread (ideally sourdough, Italian, or French bread) with a clove of garlic, cut in half. Or partially slice a baguette, evenly spaced, stud the spaces with whole or halved cloves of garlic, and briefly bake in the oven—even better, if you also add a few dabs of butter into the slots.

Marinated Feta Cheese

5 cloves garlic
1 tsp dried thyme
1 tsp dried oregano
1/2 bunch fresh basil
1/2 bunch fresh Italian
  parsley
1/2 cup extra-virgin olive
  oil
Salt to taste
Freshly ground black
  pepper to taste
18 oz sheep's-milk feta
  cheese, cut into 2 slices

Prep time: about 1 hour and 15
minutes
Entire recipe:
2200 calories/73 g protein
210 g fat/7 g carbohydrates

1 Peel the garlic, and mince, and add to a bowl. Mix in the thyme and the oregano.

2 Rinse the basil and the parsley, shake dry, remove the stems, and chop the leaves finely. Stir the leaves, along with the oil, into the garlic. Season with salt and pepper.

3 Place the slices of cheese next to each other in a bowl, and distribute the marinade on the cheese. Allow the cheese to stand, covered, in the refrigerator for at least 1 hour, turning it twice.

Garlicky Cherry Tomatoes

A delicious little gift from the kitchen. It keeps for 6 months, and goes with savory foods, and works as an hors d'oeuvre.

Ingredients for 3-cup jar:

18 oz cherry tomatoes (red
  and gold, if possible)
10 cloves garlic
3/4 cups white wine
  vinegar
1/2 cup water
1 tbs green peppercorns
1 sprig fresh oregano (or
  1 tsp dried)
1 tsp salt

Prep time: about 15 minutes
Entire recipe:
150 calories/8 g protein
1 g fat/28 g carbohydrates

1 Wash and dry the tomatoes well.

2 Peel the garlic, cut in half lengthwise, and layer them in a jar, alternating with the tomatoes.

3 Put the vinegar, water, peppercorns, oregano, and salt in a pot, and bring to boiling. Pour the hot fluid over the tomatoes, and close the jar.

Camembert-Garlic Spread

Serves 4:
10 oz ripe Camembert
  cheese, rind removed
2 oz soft butter
4 cloves garlic
2 tbs dry white wine
Salt to taste
Freshly ground black
  pepper to taste
A pinch of freshly grated
  nutmeg
1 tbs chopped green
  pistachios

Prep time: about 10 minutes
Per serving: 330 calories
17 g protein/29 g fat
2 g carbohydrates

1 Mash the Camembert with a fork, and mix with the butter in a bowl.

2 Peel the garlic, mince, and add to the bowl. Mix in the white wine, and season with the salt, pepper, and nutmeg.

3 Finally, mix in the pistachios. Refrigerate until ready to serve.

Marinated Feta Cheese (above) and Camembert-Garlic Spread (below). The marinated Garlicky Cherry Tomatoes make a delicious little gift.

Herbed Garlic

A nice addition to salad dishes. It also goes well with broiled and roasted foods, especially lamb.

Tip! For this recipe you should use very fresh garlic, which is aromatic, but not too intense.

Serves 4:
5 heads of fresh garlic
3 tbs butter
1/4 cup olive oil
2 sprigs fresh rosemary
2 sprigs fresh thyme
1 bay leaf
1/2 tsp salt
1 tsp freshly ground black pepper
1/2 cup dry white wine

Prep time: about 30 minutes
Per serving: 260 calories
5 g protein/14 g fat
22 g carbohydrates

1 Separate the garlic heads into cloves, and peel the cloves.

2 In a wide pot, heat the butter to foaming, add the olive oil, and heat.

3 Add the garlic cloves, and stir.

4 Mix in the rosemary, thyme, and bay leaf. Season with salt and pepper, and sauté everything for about 3 minutes. Then add the white wine, cover, and simmer an additional 15 minutes, until the garlic is soft.

Sweet & Sour Garlic

Ingredients for 4 jars (1-cup size):
20 medium heads of fresh garlic
2 tbs salt
1 cup white wine vinegar
2 cups dry white wine
1 cup water
2 bay leaves
1 sprig fresh thyme
1 sprig fresh rosemary
1 sprig fresh oregano
1/4 cup honey
2 tbs pink peppercorns
2 tbs green peppercorns
1 cup or more extra-virgin olive oil

Prep time: about 1 hour and 20 minutes
Per jar: 600 calories
18 g protein/13 g fat
93 g carbohydrates

1 Separate the garlic heads into cloves, and peel the cloves. Put the garlic cloves in a pot, and cover them with water. Sprinkle with 1 tbs salt, and slowly bring to a boil. Then pour off the water, and allow the garlic to cool completely.

2 Meanwhile, mix the remaining 1 tbs salt, the vinegar, and the white wine in a pot. Add the water, bay leaves, thyme, rosemary, and oregano, and stir in the honey. Bring the liquid to a boil, and simmer gently for about 10 minutes. Meanwhile rinse the jars with boiling water.

3 Put the garlic cloves into the jars, and sprinkle the pink and green peppercorns over them. Pour the hot liquid through a sieve into the jars, so that the garlic cloves are well covered with the liquid. Allow to cool completely. Then pour the olive oil on top to make a thick layer.

4 Close the jars, and allow to marinate in the refrigerator for at least 4 weeks.

Herbed Garlic (left) and
Sweet & Sour Garlic (right)

Garlic-Herb Bread Wreath

This substantial bread wreath is perfect for picnics, parties, or for a leisurely Sunday brunch with family or friends. You'll be tempted to eat it while it's still hot, but it's really much better lukewarm or cool.

Serves 8:
Makes one 10-inch wreath
For the dough:
2 2/3 cups flour
1 pkg (about 1 tbs) rapid-
  rise yeast
1 tsp sugar
A pinch of salt
Scant 1 cup lukewarm milk
4 oz butter
For the filling:
1 bunch each: fresh chives,
  basil, and Italian parsley
1/2 bunch green onions
10 oz feta cheese
3 egg yolks
1 egg
2/3 cup crème fraîche
8 cloves garlic
Freshly ground black
  pepper
For the pan:
Vegetable oil
2 egg yolks for brushing

Prep time: About 2 hours and 30 minutes
Per serving: 520 calories
6 g protein/32 g fat
42 g carbohydrates

1 For the dough, put the flour, yeast, sugar, and salt in the bowl of a food processor and pulse with the dough blade or metal blade until blended. Add the milk and process until the mixture forms a smooth dough. Continue to process for about 2 minutes.

2 Add the butter, cut into cubes and process until the butter is incorporated. Transfer the dough to a bowl, cover loosely with plastic wrap, and let rise for about 1 hour, until the dough has doubled in bulk.

3 For the filling, rinse the herbs, shake them dry, and chop finely. Trim and wash the green onions, and slice them finely.

4 Preheat the oven to 350°F.

5 Crumble the feta cheese into a bowl, and mix it with the herbs, green onions, egg yolks, egg, and crème fraîche. Peel the garlic, mince, and mix it with the herb mixture. Season with pepper.

6 Punch down the risen dough and transfer it to a floured work surface. With a floured rolling pin, roll out the dough, shaping it to make a thin, long rectangle. Spread the filling over the dough, leaving about a 1 1/2-inch border. Carefully roll up the dough, starting from the long end.

7 Grease a 10-inch tube pan with vegetable oil and place the roll inside. Pinch together the ends of the roll to form a wreath. Stir the egg yolks, and brush the wreath evenly with them. Bake the wreath in the oven (middle rack) for about an hour, until the wreath sounds hollow when tapped. If the wreath looks like it's getting too dark on the surface, cover it with aluminum foil, and continue to bake.

Variations
You can also prepare the filling with vegetables. Reduce the feta cheese to 8 oz, and decrease the amount of herbs by half. Grate 1 zucchini or 2 peeled carrots, and sauté them in 2 tbs butter for about 8 minutes. Season the vegetables with salt and pepper, and mix with the crumbled cheese.
Instead of feta cheese, you can also use a strong Roquefort, or use equal amounts of both kinds of cheeses. If you like it very substantial, you can mix cooked bacon or strips of salami (about 4 oz) with the vegetables.

Vegetables and Salads

Tabbouleh

A salad-like variation of the Tunisian national meal, this dish is ideal for parties.

Serves 4:
2 lemons
2 tbs olive oil
1 cup tomato juice
6–8 cloves garlic
** (depending on size)**
8 oz instant couscous
1 cucumber
1 yellow bell pepper
2 large tomatoes
Salt to taste
Freshly ground black
** pepper to taste**
Hot paprika
1/2 bunch fresh mint

Prep time: about 50 minutes
Per serving: 260 calories
8 g protein/6 g fat
39 g carbohydrates

1 Squeeze the lemons, and mix the juice with the olive oil and tomato juice in a large bowl. Peel the garlic, press through garlic press, and add to the bowl.

2 Stir the couscous into this mixture, and allow to stand for about 30 minutes.

3 Peel the cucumber and cut it into small cubes. Wash the yellow bell pepper, remove the seeds and veins, and cut into cubes as well. Briefly plunge the tomatoes into boiling water, remove the skin, stem, and seeds, and then cut the tomato flesh into small cubes.

4 Mix the vegetables into the couscous, season with salt and pepper, and some paprika.

5 Rinse the mint, remove the stems, and mix the leaves into the salad.

Colorful Couscous Salad

A salad-like variation of the Tunisian national meal, this dish is ideal for parties.

Serves 4:
2 lemons
2 tbs olive oil
1 cup tomato juice
6–8 cloves garlic
  (depending on size)
8 oz instant couscous
1 cucumber
1 yellow bell pepper
2 large tomatoes
Salt to taste
Freshly ground black
  pepper to taste
Hot paprika
1/2 bunch fresh mint

Prep time: about 50 minutes
Per serving: 260 calories
8 g protein/6 g fat
39 g carbohydrates

1 Squeeze the lemons, and mix the juice with the olive oil and tomato juice in a large bowl. Peel the garlic, press through garlic press, and add to the bowl.

2 Stir the couscous into this mixture, and allow to stand for about 30 minutes.

3 Peel the cucumber and cut it into small cubes. Wash the yellow bell pepper, remove the seeds and veins, and cut into cubes as well. Briefly plunge the tomatoes into boiling water, remove the skin, stem, and seeds, and then cut the tomato flesh into small cubes.

4 Mix the vegetables into the couscous, season with salt and pepper, and some paprika.

5 Rinse the mint, remove the stems, and mix the leaves into the salad.

Crisp Salad with Mushrooms

Serve as an hors d'oeuvre or a light entrée.

Serves 4:
1 medium head iceberg
  lettuce
1/4 cup white wine
  vinegar
Salt to taste
Freshly ground pepper to
  taste
1 pinch Dijon-style
  mustard
3 tbs vegetable oil
6 oz mushrooms
2 tbs butter
5 cloves garlic
1/2 handful fresh chervil
  (optional)

Prep time: about 30 minutes
Per serving: 140 calories
2 g protein/14 g fat
3 g carbohydrates

1 Wash the lettuce leaves, break them apart, and drain them well.

2 In a large bowl, whisk together the vinegar, salt, pepper, mustard, and the oil to make a creamy dressing. Add the lettuce, and toss it in the dressing.

3 Trim the mushrooms, rinse, and slice very thin. Heat the butter in a pan, and sauté the mushrooms over medium-high heat for about 5 minutes.

4 Peel the garlic, press through garlic press, and add to the pan. Season the mushrooms with salt and pepper, and sprinkle over the lettuce while warm.

5 Rinse the chervil, if using, pinch off the stems, and sprinkle the leaves over the lettuce. Best served with fresh bread.

Warm Lentil Salad

Serves 4:
1 onion
1 whole clove
1 bay leaf
10 oz lentils
4 cloves garlic
2 large tomatoes
1/2 bunch green onions
1 tsp salt
1/4 cup red wine vinegar
Freshly ground black
  pepper to taste
5 tbs olive oil

Soaking time: 12 hours
Prep time: 40–50 minutes
Per serving: 310 calories
16 g protein/11 g fat
38 g carbohydrates

1 Peel the onion, and stud it with the clove and bay leaf, and put it in a saucepan. Cover the lentils with water. Smash 2 unpeeled garlic cloves slightly with a knife blade, and add to the pot. Bring everything to a boil, reduce the heat, and simmer for 30–40 minutes until the lentils are soft. Check occasionally for tenderness.

2 Briefly plunge the tomatoes into boiling water, skin them, cut in half crosswise, remove the seeds and stem, and cut the tomatoes into small cubes. Wash the green onions, and slice them, making very fine rings.

3 Stir a little salt into the vinegar, add pepper, and add olive oil very slowly in a fine stream, while beating it with a wire whisk until the dressing is creamy. Add the remaining garlic cloves, pressing it though a garlic press.

4 Drain the lentils, and while still warm, toss them with the tomatoes and the green onions in the dressing.

White Beans with Garlic Foam

Serves 4:
2 cans (15 oz each) small
  white beans
3 tbs walnut oil
Juice of 2 lemons
Salt to taste
A pinch of cayenne pepper
Freshly ground black
  pepper to taste
2 eggs
1 egg yolk
1 cup cold chicken stock
2 cloves garlic
A pinch of freshly grated
  nutmeg
10 oz boneless smoked
  ham, finely sliced
1 sprig fresh tarragon

Prep time: about 30 minutes
Per serving: 1300 calories
98 g protein/21 g fat
180 g carbohydrates

1 Rinse the beans in a colander and drain well.

2 In a bowl, stir together the walnut oil with 1/4 cup of the lemon juice, the salt, cayenne pepper, and black pepper. Add the beans, toss well, and let marinate.

3 In a bowl, stir together the eggs and the egg yolk with a little bit of the stock. Mince the garlic and stir it into the egg mixture.

4 Put the remaining stock and the rest of the lemon juice in a heatproof bowl set over a pot of simmering water (be sure that the bottom of the bowl does not touch the water). Slowly pour the egg mixture into the bowl, whisking constantly. Heat, whisking, until a creamy, thickened foam is obtained. Season with salt, pepper, and the nutmeg.

5 Cut the ham into strips, and toss it with the beans.

6 Divide the garlic foam among 4 serving plates. Divide the beans among the plates on top of the foam. Rinse the tarragon, pick off the leaves, and sprinkle them on top for garnish.

Photo above: Warm Lentil Salad
Photo below: White Beans with Garlic Foam

Crispy Mushrooms with Avocado-Garlic Dip

The crisp mushrooms are a perfect complement to the spicy dressing. They make a sophisticated snack, or light meal.

Serves 4:
For the dip:

1 ripe avocado
Juice of 1/2 lemon
5 cloves garlic
6 oz plain yogurt
Salt to taste
Freshly ground white
  pepper to taste
A pinch of cayenne pepper
1 bunch chives
For the mushrooms:
6 oz brown or small white
  mushrooms
2 eggs
Salt to taste
A pinch of Freshly ground
  black pepper
A pinch of freshly grated
  nutmeg
1 tsp soy sauce
1/4 cup flour
3 1/2 oz fine dry bread
  crumbs (preferably panko)
For frying:
4 cups vegetable oil

Prep time: about 30 minutes
Per serving: 550 calories
14 g protein/42 g fat
30 g carbohydrates

1 For the dip, cut the avocado in half lengthwise, remove the pit, and scrape the avocado out of the peel.

Immediately drizzle lemon juice on it.

2 Peel the garlic cloves, and puree them, along with the avocado and the yogurt, in a blender. Season the dip with salt, white pepper, and the cayenne pepper.

3 Rinse the chives, shake dry, slice finely, and mix them into the dip. Refrigerate the dip.

4 Rinse the mushrooms, trim, and pat them dry.

5 Beat the eggs, and season with the salt, pepper, nutmeg, and soy sauce. Put the flour, and the bread crumbs each on a separate plate.

6 Heat the oil in a deep, wide pot or a deep-fat fryer.

7 Coat the mushrooms first in the flour, then in the eggs, and finally with the bread crumbs, shaking off the excess between steps.

8 Deep-fry the mushrooms, one serving at a time, for about 1 minute, until golden brown. Let the mushrooms drain on paper towels, and serve with the avocado dip.

Variations
You can use broccoli and cauliflower florets instead of, or in addition to, the mushrooms. They must first be cooked until tender-crisp in salted water and dried very well (to prevent spattering).

> **Tip!** The avocado garlic dip is also great as a fondue dipping sauce, or served alongside broiled food.

Crispy Mushrooms with Avocado-Garlic Dip

Peperonata

This braised vegetable mix is delicious, warm or cold, as a main course, or as a side dish.

Serves 4:
10 oz onions
3 tbs olive oil
4 cloves garlic
8 oz each red, green, and yellow bell peppers
24 oz large tomatoes
1 bay leaf
1 sprig fresh rosemary (or 1 tsp dried)
Salt to taste
Freshly ground black pepper to taste

Prep time: about 1 hour
Per serving: 140 calories
5 g protein/7 g fat
14 g carbohydrates

1 Peel the onions, and slice finely.

2 Heat the olive oil in a wide pan, sauté the onion rings until translucent.

3 Peel the garlic, press through garlic press, and add to the onions in pan.

4 Wash the bell peppers, remove the seeds and thick ribs inside, cut into 1/2-inch wide strips, and add to the pan.

5 Briefly plunge the tomatoes into boiling water, skin them, cut into eighths, remove seeds, and mix in with pan ingredients. Add the bay leaf and rosemary. Add salt and pepper, and simmer, over very low heat, covered, for about 30 minutes, stirring occasionally.

6 Finally, remove the bay leaf and rosemary sprig. Season again with salt and pepper.

Savory Mixed Mushrooms

This dish goes well with noodles, little dumplings, or potatoes boiled in their jackets.

Serves 4:
8 oz oyster mushrooms
8 oz brown mushrooms
8 oz small white mushrooms
1 large onion
2 tbs butter
3 cloves garlic
Salt to taste
Freshly ground black pepper to taste
2/3 cup crème fraîche
1/2 bunch fresh Italian parsley

Prep time: about 35 minutes
Per serving: 230 calories
5 g protein/22 g fat
4 g carbohydrates

1 Trim the mushrooms, and clean them with paper towels or a mushroom brush. Slice the oyster mushrooms into narrow strips, and the other mushrooms into very thin slices.

2 Peel the onion, and chop finely. Heat the butter in a large pan, and sauté the onion until it becomes soft.

3 Add the mushrooms, and cook briefly over high heat. Then reduce the heat.

4. Peel the garlic, press through garlic press, and add to the pan. Season the mushrooms with salt and pepper, stir in the crème fraîche, and allow everything to simmer, over very low heat, for about 10 minutes.

5 Rinse the parsley, shake dry, chop medium finely, and mix it in just before serving.

Below: Peperonata
Above: Savory Mixed Mushrooms

Potato–Eggplant Ragout

Serves 4:
2 onions
3 tbs olive oil
14 oz eggplants
20 oz potatoes
1/2 cup vegetable stock
5 cloves garlic
3 tsp curry powder
Salt to taste
Freshly ground black
  pepper to taste
2 tbs fresh oregano leaves
  (or 1 tbs dried)

Prep time: about 1 hour
Per serving: 200 calories
5 g protein/7 g fat
31 g carbohydrates

1 Peel the onions, and chop finely.

2 Heat the olive oil in a large pan, and sauté the onions until translucent.

3 Wash the eggplants, remove the stems, and cut into cubes of about 1/2 inch. Peel the potatoes, wash, and cube them in the same manner. Put the eggplant and potato cubes in the skillet, stir to mix. Pour in the vegetable stock.

4 Peel the garlic, press it through a garlic press, and add to the pan. Season the vegetables with the curry, salt, and pepper, and cover, and simmer over low heat, for about 30 minutes, stirring occasionally.

5 Check seasoning, adding more if needed, and sprinkle the oregano on top.

Spring Vegetable Sauté

Serves 4:
8 oz kohlrabi
12 oz baby carrots
8 oz snow peas
6 oz fresh spinach
1/2 bunch green onions
3 cloves garlic
3 tbs butter
Salt to taste
Freshly ground black
  pepper to taste
1/2 cup vegetable stock
5 tbs herbed cream cheese
Juice of 1/2 lemon
1 handful fresh chervil

Prep time: about 45 minutes
Per serving: 190 calories
7 g protein/13 g fat
12 g carbohydrates

1 Peel the kohlrabi and the carrots, cut them into cubes of about 1/4 inch. Wash the snow peas and cut them into diamond-shaped pieces. Wash the spinach, drain well, and remove the stems. Trim and wash the green onions, and slice fine rings. Peel the garlic.

2 Heat the butter in a pan. Press the garlic through a garlic press, and add to the pan. Add the carrots and the kohlrabi, and sauté for about 4 minutes, stirring frequently.

3 Mix in the snow peas, the spinach, and the onions. Season with salt and pepper. Add the vegetable stock, bring to a boil, and then simmer, covered, for about 15 minutes.

4 Stir the cream cheese with the lemon juice until smooth, and mix it into the vegetables. Check the seasoning again.

5 Rinse the chervil, remove the stems, and sprinkle the leaves on the vegetables. Serve with new potatoes or rice, or as a side dish.

Above: Potato–Eggplant Ragout
Below: Spring Vegetable Sauté

Meat and Poultry

Poultry Terrine with Mascarpone

Terrines are great summer fare, or served as an hors d'oeuvre, and they are very popular on party buffets, and for Sunday brunches. This poultry terrine is easily prepared, and will be a success even for beginners.

Serves 8:
Ingredients for 1 terrine dish (1–quart size):
2 egg yolks
Salt to taste
Freshly ground white
   pepper to taste
A pinch of cayenne pepper
Juice of 1/2 lemon
6 cloves garlic
12 oz mascarpone cheese
1/2 bunch fresh basil
1 bunches each: fresh
   chives and Italian parsley
28 oz ground turkey
4 small boneless skinless
   chicken breast halves
Freshly ground black
   pepper to taste
2 tbs butter
To grease mold:

vegetable oil

Prep time: about 1 hour and 45
minutes
Per serving: 406 calories
38 g protein/25 g fat
1 g carbohydrate

1 In a large bowl, stir together the egg yolks with salt, white pepper, cayenne pepper, and the lemon juice, mixing well.

2 Peel the garlic, press through a press, and add to the bowl.

3 Add the mascarpone cheese, a tablespoon at a time, stirring continuously. Rinse the herbs. Pick the basil and parsley leaves off, chop all the herbs fine, and mix them, along with the ground turkey into the mascarpone mixture. Check seasoning, and adjust, if necessary. Preheat oven to 350° F.

4 Sprinkle the chicken breasts with salt and pepper. Heat half of the butter in a pan over medium-high heat. Sear the chicken breasts on all sides then allow to cool a bit.

5 Grease the terrine mold well with oil , and fill with half of the turkey mixture. Arrange the chicken breasts on top, then cover with the rest of the turkey mixture.

6 Place the dish in a roasting pan. Fill the roasting pan with hot water, so that the bottom half of the terrine dish stands in water. Place the roasting pan in the oven (middle rack), and bake the terrine for about 1 hour.

7 Let the terrine dish cool completely. Once cooled, turn the terrine upside down onto a platter. Slice it, and serve. A mixed green salad is a nice companion.

Variations

You can also mix mushrooms into the turkey mixture. Best suited are brown, white, or oyster mushrooms. Trim and rub clean with paper towels about 5 oz of the mushrooms of your choice. Slice them, or, in case you use oyster mushrooms, cut them into strips. Then sauté them in hot butter, until all the liquid is evaporated. Season with salt, pepper, and a pinch of freshly grated nutmeg. Let cool a bit, and mix into the ground meat mixture. Then continue preparing the terrine as described.

Chicken Breasts with Pistachio Sauce

Serves 4:
8 boneless, skinless
  chicken breast halves,
  each about 4 oz
Freshly ground white
  pepper to taste
1/2 cup extra-virgin olive
  oil
Juice of 1 lemon, plus
  more to taste
8 cloves garlic
1/2 bunch fresh basil
Salt to taste
About 2 ounce shelled
  pistachios, ground
1 tbs bread crumbs

Prep time: about 2 hours and 30
minutes
Per serving: 400 calories
61 g protein/16 g fat
6 g carbohydrates

1 Sprinkle the chicken breasts with pepper, and place them on a platter in one layer.

2 Mix the olive oil with the juice of 1 lemon. Peel the garlic, mince, and add to the olive oil and lemon juice. Rinse the basil, pick the leaves off the stems, cut them into fine strips, and add to the marinade (save a few strips for garnish).

3 Pour the marinade over the chicken breasts, and let stand, covered, in the refrigerator for about 2 hours, turning occasionally.

4 Take the chicken breasts out of the marinade and brush off the basil; set the marinade aside. Season the chicken with salt and pepper.

5 Sear the chicken breasts in a nonstick skillet on both sides, then simmer covered, over low heat, for 8-10 minutes. Remove the chicken from the pan and keep warm.

6 Strain the marinade into the skillet and bring to a boil for about 1 minute. Remove from the heat and mix in the pistachios and bread crumbs to make a sauce. Season with salt, pepper and more lemon juice if desired.

7 Slice the chicken breasts against the grain, and arrange like a fan, each with a dollop of the sauce. Garnish with the reserved basil. Serve any remaining sauce separately.

Garlic Chicken with Apple Cider

Serves 4:
1 small chicken (about 3
  pounds)
Salt to taste
Freshly ground black
  pepper to taste
Flour
1/4 cup olive oil
15–20 cloves garlic
  (depending on size)
2 cups apple cider
1 bunch green onions
A pinch of cayenne pepper

Prep time: about 1 hour and 30
minutes
Per serving: 570 calories
63 g protein/25 g fat
21 g carbohydrates

1 Cut the chicken into serving pieces, and remove the skin. Sprinkle salt and pepper on the pieces, and dredge them in flour, shaking off the excess.

2 Heat the olive oil in a deep skillet. Sear the chicken pieces on all sides, and take them out of the pan.

3 Peel the garlic cloves, and simmer them in the oil until just golden.

4 Place the chicken pieces back in the pan, ideally in one layer. Add the apple cider, and simmer, covered, over low heat, for about 20 minutes.

5 Trim and wash the green onions, and place them in the pan after about 25 minutes.

6 Remove the chicken and onions from the pan, and keep them warm. Stir the pan juices, skimming off the fat, and season with salt, black pepper, and cayenne pepper.

7 Put the chicken pieces on a platter, pour the pan juices over them, and garnish with the green onions.

Garlic Chicken with Apple Cider (top) and Chicken Breasts with Pistachio Sauce (bottom).

Veal Roast with Corn Crust

The meat stays nice and juicy under the delicious protective coating.

Serves 4:
1 boneless veal rump roast, about 2 lb
Salt to taste
Freshly ground white pepper to taste
Freshly grated nutmeg to taste
2 tbs olive oil
2 medium onions
2 medium carrots
1 small can corn kernels (about 7 oz)
5–6 cloves garlic
1/2 bunch fresh Italian parsley
2 tbs bread crumbs
1 tsp grated lemon zest
2 tbs butter
Juice of 1/2 lemon
1/2 cup beef stock
5 oz crème fraîche

Prep time: about 1 hour and 30 minutes
Per serving: 500 calories
45 g protein/29 g fat
16 g carbohydrates

1. Rinse the meat with cold water, pat dry, and rub on all sides with the salt, pepper, and nutmeg.

2. Heat the oil in a Dutch oven over medium–high heat, and sear the meat on all sides.

3. Preheat the oven to 425° F.

4. Peel the onions and the carrots, and chop finely. Sprinkle them around the meat.

5. Place the pan on a rack in the middle of the oven, reduce the oven heat to 350°F, and roast the meat for about 45 minutes.

6. Drain the corn kernels in a sieve. Peel the garlic cloves, and puree them, along with the corn in a food processor or blender.

7. Rinse the parsley, pick the leaves off the stems, chop the leaves finely, and mix, along with the bread crumbs and the grated lemon peel into the puree. Season with salt, pepper, and nutmeg.

8. Take the meat from the oven, and set it on a baking sheet, which is covered with aluminum foil. Increase the oven heat to broil. Spread the corn paste on top of the roast evenly. Put dabs of butter on the corn paste,

and broil the meat for about 8 minutes, until the crust is crisp. Allow the roast to stand in the turned-off oven for about 10 minutes.

9. Meanwhile, put the vegetables, along with the roast drippings, the lemon juice, the beef stock, and the crème fraîche in the food processor or blender, and puree. Simmer the sauce in a saucepan until desired consistency is obtained, and check seasoning.

10. Cut the roast in slices about 1/2-inch thick, and serve with the sauce. Steamed vegetables and noodles are suitable side dishes.

Variation

If you don't want to make a large roast, you can put the corn mixture on steaks. In that case, sear the steaks on both sides, season with salt and pepper, and spread the paste on top. Then cook the steaks under the broiler until desired doneness.

Tip! The corn mixture can also be used as a side dish for fish, meat, or poultry. If you like it heartier, you can mix in fried strips of bacon.

Veal Roast with Corn Crust

Stuffed Turkey Cutlets

Serves 4:
1/2 bunch fresh Italian
  parsley
4 cloves garlic
1 tbs olive oil
6 oz mozzarella cheese
Salt to taste
Freshly ground black
  pepper to taste
4 turkey cutlets, each
  about 4 1/2 oz
2 tbs butter
1 lemon
Wooden toothpicks

Prep time: about 35 minutes
Per serving: 310 calories
89 g protein/17 g fat
1 g carbohydrate

1 Rinse the parsley, shake dry, and chop the leaves. Put them in a small bowl. Peel the garlic, press though a garlic press, and add it to the bowl. Add the olive oil, and mix everything.

2 Cut the mozzarella into 8 slices, sprinkle salt and pepper on both sides. Spread the herb mixture on 4 slices, and put the remaining slices on top.

3 Sprinkle salt and pepper on the turkey cutlets. Place the mozzarella packages on top, and fold the meat over them. Secure the packets together with toothpicks.

4 Heat the butter in a skillet over medium-high heat, and sear the cutlets on both sides for about 5 minutes. Reduce the heat to medium and continue sautéing for about 8 minutes, until the meat is cooked through.

5 Cut the lemon lengthwise into quarters, and garnish the stuffed turkey cutlets with them. These go well with a warm baguette, or fried potatoes.

Veal Rolls in Lemon Cream

These are also good served cold.

Serves 4:
8 cloves garlic
3 oz Parmesan cheese,
  freshly grated
5 tbs olive oil
1/2 bunch fresh mint
8 thin veal cutlets, about
  4 oz each
Salt to taste
Freshly ground black
  pepper to taste
Cayenne pepper
1/2 cup dry white wine
Juice of 2 lemons
1 cup heavy cream

Prep time: about 1 hour and 10
minutes
Per serving: 690 calories
59 g protein/45 g fat
7 g carbohydrates

1 Peel the garlic cloves, and mince, and add to a bowl. Add the Parmesan cheese, and 3 tbs of the olive oil.

2 Rinse the mint, shake dry, and pick off the leaves. Set aside 4 leaves for garnish.

3 Sprinkle the cutlets on both sides with salt, pepper and cayenne pepper, and spread the cheese mixture on one side. Place the mint leaves on top, and form the meat into rolls. Secure the rolls with kitchen string.

4 Heat the remaining 2 tbs olive oil in a skillet, and sear the veal rolls on all sides, then take them out of the pan. Pour the fat away, and stir the pan drippings with the white wine and the lemon juice. Stir in the cream, bring to a boil briefly, and add the rolls to the pan. Cook, covered, for about 35 minutes, over low heat, until done.

5 Take the rolls out of the pan, and keep them warm. Cook the sauce until the desired consistency is obtained, and season with salt, pepper, and cayenne pepper.

6 Serve the veal rolls with the sauce, and garnish with the remaining mint. Goes well with noodles, or rice, mixed with almonds.

Below: Veal Rolls in Lemon
Cream
Above: Stuffed Turkey
Cutlets.

Beef Rolls with Oyster Mushrooms

Serves 4:
1 onion
About 2 oz bacon
1 tbs olive oil
7 oz oyster mushrooms
4–6 cloves garlic
Salt to taste
Freshly ground black
  pepper to taste
1/2 bunch fresh Italian
  parsley
2 egg yolks
4 thin slices beef round,
  about 5 oz each,
  pounded thinly
2 tbs butter
1 cup dry red wine
1/2 cup heavy cream
Wooden toothpicks

Prep time: about 2 hours and 30
minutes
Per serving: 620 calories
36 g protein/46 g fat
5 g carbohydrates

1 Peel the onion, and chop finely. Cut the bacon into small cubes.

2 In a large skillet, heat the oil over medium heat, and sauté the onions, and the bacon until the onions are translucent.

3 Meanwhile trim the oyster mushrooms, and cut them in narrow, short strips. Add to the pan and sauté until almost all the liquid has evaporated.

4 Add the garlic, pressing it through a garlic press, then season everything with salt and pepper.

5 Rinse the parsley, pick off the leaves, chop them finely, and add them to the pan. Remove the pan from the heat, and let the mixture cool. Stir in the egg yolks.

6 Sprinkle salt and pepper on the beef slices. Place the mushroom filling on top. Tuck the sides in, and roll up the meat around the filling. Secure the rolls together with toothpicks.

7 In a skillet, heat the butter over medium-high heat, and sear the roulades on all sides . Add the red wine, cover, and simmer over low heat for about 1 1/2 hours. Remove the beef rolls from the pan and keep warm.

8 Stir the cream into the sauce with a wire whisk, cook about 5 minutes, and check seasoning. Serve the beef rolls with the sauce.

Pork Cutlets Baked in Foil

Serves 4:
1 medium onion
6 cloves garlic
1 tbs butter
2 large tomatoes (about
  9 oz)
1 bunch fresh Italian
  parsley
Salt to taste
Freshly ground black
  pepper to taste
2 tbs vegetable oil
4 pork cutlets

Prep time: about 1 hour
Per serving: 480 calories
40 g protein/33 g fat
7 g carbohydrates

1 Chop the onion and garlic very finely.

2 Heat the butter in a skillet, and sauté the onions over low heat until they become soft, not brown.

3 Meanwhile, briefly plunge the tomatoes into boiling water, remove the skins and seeds, and chop the flesh into fine cubes. Preheat the oven to 400° F.

4 Chop the parsley finely. Mix with the garlic-onion mixture and the tomatoes, and season with salt and pepper.

5 Heat the oil in a skillet over medium-high heat, and sear the cutlets on both sides. Season with salt and pepper.

6 Lay out 4 pieces of aluminum foil with the shiny side up. Place one cutlet on each, cover with the tomato mixture, and wrap loosely with the foil. Pinch together at the seams.

7 Set the packages on a baking sheet, and bake in the oven (middle rack) for 20–25 minutes, until cooked through. Goes well with a colorful Greek salad.

**Above: Beef Rolls with Oyster Mushrooms
Below: Pork Cutlets Baked in Foil**

Lamb Cutlets with Garlic Sabayon

The garlic sabayon also tastes delicious with steamed fish.

Serves 4:
For the vegetables:
1 each: large red, yellow, and green bell pepper
2 shallots
2 tbs butter
Salt to taste
Freshly ground white pepper to taste
For the sabayon:
3 egg yolks
Salt to taste
3 cloves garlic
1/2 cup white wine
1 cup beef stock
Lemon juice
Freshly ground white pepper to taste
For the cutlets:
2 tbs olive oil
8 lamb cutlets
Salt to taste
Freshly ground white pepper to taste
For Garnish:
A few sprigs of fresh mint

Prep time: about 50 minutes
Per serving: 900 calories
35 g protein/79 g fat
9 g carbohydrates

1 Trim the bell peppers, wash, and cut into very small cubes. Chop the shallots finely.

2 Heat the butter in a skillet, and sauté the bell peppers and shallots over low heat for about 7 minutes. Add salt and white pepper, and keep the mixture warm.

3 In the meantime, stir the egg yolks with a little salt in a bowl. Peel the garlic, press through garlic press, and add to the yolks. Place the bowl into a gently simmering double boiler, and, with a hand mixer, whisk the egg yolks until they are foamy.

4 Very slowly, add the white wine and the stock, stirring constantly, until the sauce is creamy. Careful: do not let the water boil, so as not to curdle the egg yolks.

5 Season the sauce with lemon juice and white pepper, and keep it warm.

6 Heat the olive oil in a skillet. Sauté the cutlets on both sides for about 2–3 minutes, and season with salt and white pepper.

7 Place the cutlets on pre-heated plates, and serve with a little sabayon and the peppers.

8 Rinse mint, shake dry, and add as a garnish.

Variation
Instead of lamb cutlets, equally well suited for the sabayon are fried chicken breasts or steamed fish. You can also serve fresh spinach or steamed zucchini slices as a vegetable.

Rabbit in Basil Sauce

Rabbit can be found in butcher stores. You can have it cut into serving-size pieces, or just purchase the individual pieces you prefer.

Serves 4–6:
1 rabbit, about 4 1/2 lb (have the butcher cut it into serving pieces)
Salt to taste
Freshly ground black pepper to taste
3 tbs olive oil
1 head of garlic
About 1 1/2 cups heavy cream
1 bay leaf
1 sprig fresh rosemary (or 2 tsp dried)
4 oz black olives (pitted)
1 bunch fresh basil

Prep time: about 1 hour and 15 minutes
For 6, per serving: 670 calories
54 g protein/49 g fat
5 g carbohydrates

1 Rinse the rabbit with cold water, pat dry, and rub it with salt and pepper.

2 Heat the olive oil in a skillet over medium-high heat, and sear the rabbit pieces until golden brown, then take them out of the pan.

3 Rinse the garlic head, pat dry, and cut crosswise in slices about 1/4-inch thick. Sauté them until golden brown in the olive oil, and return the rabbit pieces to the pan. Add the heavy cream, bay leaf, and rosemary. Cover, and cook for about 45 minutes over medium heat. After about 30 minutes, add the olives.

4 Rinse the basil, shake dry, and pick the leaves off the stems. Leave small leaves whole, or cut large ones into narrow strips. Sprinkle all, save a few beautiful leaves, into the pot 5 minutes before the rabbit is done.

5 Check the seasoning. Sprinkle the remaining basil leaves on top. It is best to bring the dish to the table and serve it right from the pot, family style. Serve the rabbit with pasta, baked potatoes, or simply with bread. It is excellent with sautéed zucchini and tomatoes, or a colorful salad with everything the garden offers.

Variation
Instead of heavy cream, you can use tomatoes to prepare the rabbit. Use 26 oz ripe large tomatoes. Briefly plunge them into boiling water, remove the skin and seeds, and chop. Put them in a skillet, before you cook the rabbit. The tomatoes combine very well with the garlic and the other spices.

Lamb Cutlets with Garlic Sabayon

Fish
and
Seafood

Mediterranean Fish Soup

The original recipe for this fish soup is from France, where it is called bourride. There the fish soup often is cooked with whole fish pieces, bones included. Here, it is easier to make—and particularly to eat—using fish fillets.

Serves 4–6:
28 oz mixed fish fillets
  (such as cod, salmon,
  and seabass)
Juice of 1 lemon
Salt to taste
1 large onion
1 carrot
2 stalks celery
2 tbs butter
28 oz large tomatoes
2 cups dry white wine
1 cup water
1 sprig fresh rosemary (or
  1 tsp dried)
1 bay leaf
Freshly ground black
  pepper to taste
4 cloves garlic
2 egg yolks
1/2 cup olive oil
1/2 bunch fresh basil

Prep time: about 1 hour and 30
minutes
For 6, per serving: 675 calories
39 g protein/41 g fat
20 g carbohydrates

1 Rinse the fish fillets in cold water, pat dry, and cut into bite-size cubes. Drizzle 2/3 of the lemon juice all around, season with salt, and refrigerate until ready to use.

2 Peel the onion, and chop very finely. Peel the carrot, and cut into tiny cubes. Rinse the celery (if necessary, if stalks are thick, remove strings), and cut into fine slices.

3 Heat the butter in a large pot. Sauté the onion, the carrots, and the celery over low heat until the onions are translucent.

4 Briefly plunge the tomatoes into boiling water, remove the skins, stems and seeds, and cut into large pieces. Put them in the pot, and add the white wine, and 1 cup water. Add the rosemary, bay leaf, salt, and pepper. Bring the mixture to a boil, then cover, and simmer over low heat for about 45 minutes.

5 When the vegetables are nearly done, peel the garlic, mince, and add to a tall bowl. Add the egg yolks, salt and pepper. Stir with a hand mixer or egg beater.

6 Then, add the olive oil very slowly in a fine stream, and continue stirring until a mayonnaise consistency is reached. Season with the remaining lemon juice.

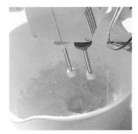

7 Stir the mayonnaise into the hot—but no longer simmering—soup. Add the fish pieces, and let them cook over very low heat for about 6 minutes, until cooked through.

8 Rinse the basil, and remove the leaves. Sprinkle them over the soup before serving.

Tip! You can prepare the fish liquid ahead of time. Just before serving, you just need to make the mayonnaise, and reheat the soup. It's an ideal meal for guests if you serve a good hors d'oeuvre, and a generous dessert.
Ideally, serve the soup in an attractive tureen, and let everyone serve themselves at the table. Serve it with warm bread.

Mackerel Baked in Foil

An inexpensive meal, easily prepared, and delicious.

Serves 4:
1 bunch fresh Italian parsley
1 red bell pepper
6 cloves garlic
1/4 cup soft butter
Salt to taste
Freshly ground black pepper to taste
4 whole mackerel or trout, each about 12 oz, cleaned, trimmed, and scales removed
Juice of 1 lemon

Prep time: about 45 minutes
Per serving: 810 calories
67 g protein/59 g fat
4 g carbohydrates

1 Rinse the parsley, shake dry, pick the leaves off the stems, and chop the leaves finely. Wash and trim the red bell pepper, and cut into very small cubes.

2 Put the red bell pepper and parsley in a small bowl. Peel the garlic, press it through a garlic press, and add to the bowl. Add the butter, and mix everything. Season with salt and pepper.

3 Preheat the oven to 350° F.

4 Rinse the fish thoroughly under cold running water, and pat dry. Drizzle the lemon juice on the fishes inside and out. Add salt and pepper, and stuff the herb mixture into the bellies.

5 Wrap the fish individually in foil, place them next to one another on a baking sheet, and bake in the oven (middle rack) for about 25 minutes.

6 Unwrap the fish, and save the juices created in baking. Skin and debone the fishes, and place on warm plates with the cooking juices and the stuffing.

Cod with Spinach Puree

Serves 4:
4 oz fresh spinach
Salt to taste
6 cloves garlic
3 tbs crème fraîche
Freshly ground black pepper to taste
A pinch of nutmeg, freshly grated
2 tbs bread crumbs
20 oz cod fillets
Juice of 1 lemon
1 tbs butter, melted

Prep time: about 50 minutes
Per serving: 200 calories
27 g protein/8 g fat
6 g carbohydrates

1. Sort the spinach, wash it very well, and pinch off the stems. Blanch it in boiling, salted water for about 2 minutes, quench it with cold water, and press to drain well.

2. Peel the garlic cloves, and puree in a food processor or blender along with the spinach, and the crème fraîche.

3. Season the mixture with salt, pepper, and the nutmeg, and mix in the bread crumbs.

4. Preheat the oven to 400° F.

5. Rinse the cod fillet in cold water, pat dry, drizzle lemon juice all around, sprinkle with salt and pepper.

6. Place a large piece of aluminum foil on a work surface, shiny side up, brush it with the butter, and put the fish on it.

7. Spread the spinach puree on top of the fish. Wrap the fish in the aluminum foil, and close the seams well. Place the package on a baking sheet.

8. Bake the fish in the oven (middle rack) for about 20 minutes, until cooked through.

Spinach Fettuccine with Salmon Sauce

Serves 4:
Salt to taste
16 oz dried spinach
  fettuccine
1 small onion
2 tbs butter
1 clove garlic
1 cup dry white wine
About 1 1/2 cups heavy
  cream
Freshly ground white
  pepper to taste
1 tbs lemon juice
12 oz fresh salmon fillet
1 bunch fresh chives

Prep time: about 30 minutes
Per serving: 1000 calories
37 g protein/52 g fat
90 g carbohydrates

1 Bring plenty of salted water to boil. Add the pasta and cook for 8-10 minutes, until slightly firm to the bite (al dente).

2 Meanwhile peel the onion, and chop it very finely. Heat the butter in a pot over medium heat, and sauté the onion until translucent. Peel the garlic, mince, and add to the pot.

3 Add the white wine, and cook until the liquid has almost evaporated. Add the heavy cream, bring to a boil, and allow it to cook in the open pot until it has evaporated by almost one third. Season with salt and white pepper, and the lemon juice.

4 Meanwhile, cut the salmon in small cubes. Rinse the chives, slice thin, and stir them and the salmon into the hot sauce, and simmer for 2-3 minutes, until the salmon is cooked through.

5 Drain the noodles, distribute on warm plates, and spoon the salmon and sauce over them in the middle.

Redfish Gratin with Mozzarella

Serves 4:
26 oz redfish fillet of
Juice of 1 lemon
Salt to taste
Freshly ground white
  pepper to taste
1/2 bunch fresh Italian
  parsley
1/2 bunch fresh dill
1 tsp fresh thyme (or 1/2
  tsp dried)
5 cloves garlic
3 tbs olive oil
20 oz large tomatoes
6 oz mozzarella cheese

Prep time: about 1 hour and 15
minutes
Per serving: 380 calories
43 g protein/19 g fat
6 g carbohydrates

1 Rinse the fish with cold, running water, and pat dry. Cut it into rather large pieces, drizzle 1 tbs lemon juice over it, and sprinkle with salt and white pepper.

2 Rinse the parsley and the dill, pick the leaves off the stems, and chop the leaves finely. Put them, along with the thyme, in a small bowl. Peel the garlic, mince, and add to the bowl. Mix in 2 tbs of the olive oil.

3 Pour the marinade over the fish, and allow to stand in the refrigerator for 20 minutes, turning once.

4 Preheat the oven to 400° F. Briefly plunge the tomatoes into boiling water, remove the skins, seeds, and stems, and slice them. Cut the mozzarella into thin slices.

5 Brush an ovenproof dish with the remaining olive oil. Alternate the fish pieces, the tomatoes, and the mozzarella, in layers like roof shingles, in the dish. Pour the marinade over all, add salt and pepper, and cover the dish tightly with aluminum foil. Bake in the oven (middle rack) for about 25 minutes, until the fish is cooked through. Remove the aluminum foil, and broil for an additional 10 minutes, until the top is lightly browned.

Roasted Whole Fish with Vegetables

A very practical dish, because, once in the oven, there is no more work to be done. Ideal for entertaining.

Serves 4:

One porgy or sea bream, about 2 lb, or other whole fish, cleaned, trimmed, and scales removed
Lemon juice
Salt to taste
Freshly ground white pepper to taste
6 cloves garlic
2 lemons
1 each: red, yellow and green bell pepper
10 oz small zucchini
18 oz large tomatoes
1/2 bunch fresh Italian parsley
1/2 cup dry white wine
1/2 cup olive oil

Prep time: about 1 hour and 15 minutes
Per serving: 670 calories
46 g protein/46 g fat
13 g carbohydrates

1 Rinse the fish in cold water, and pat dry. Drizzle lemon juice inside and out of the fish, and sprinkle with salt and white pepper.

2 Peel the garlic. Cut 3 cloves in half lengthwise. Scrub the lemon with hot water, and cut into 6 segments.

3 With a sharp knife, cut 3 notches on both sides of the fish. Put in each notch one halved garlic clove, and one lemon segment.

4 Wash and trim the red, yellow and green bell peppers, and cut strips about 1/2-inch wide.

5 Wash and trim the zucchini, and slice finely.

6 Briefly plunge the tomatoes into boiling water, remove the skin, seeds, and stems, and chop into large pieces.

7 Rinse the parsley, shake dry, pick leaves off the stems, and chop finely.

8 Preheat the oven to 400° F.

9 Put the tomatoes, the zucchini, the bell peppers, and the parsley in a bowl. Mince the remaining garlic, and add to the bowl. Mix everything. Add salt and pepper, and put the mixture in a sufficiently large baking dish as a bed for the fish. Add the white wine.

10 Place the fish on top, and pour the olive oil over it. Cover with aluminum foil, and bake in the oven (middle rack) for about 15 minutes. Remove the aluminum foil, reduce the heat to 350° F, and continue baking for an additional 25 minutes until done. If necessary, cover it up once more to prevent over-browning.

11 Remove the skin and bones from the fish, cut it into serving pieces, and serve with the vegetables.

Variations

Instead of a whole fish, you can use fillets. Cook the vegetables according to the recipe and add the fillets about halfway through the cooking time. The mixed vegetables can be replaced with sautéed oyster mushrooms, or a bed of spinach. Potatoes work well also, and are filling at the same time. Cut the potatoes in very thin slices, put them in a greased dish, and pour stock over them. Then bake them in a preheated oven at 425° F for 45–50 minutes. Then place the fish on top, and bake until the fish is done, depending on the kind of fish used.

You can serve it with a sauce of light mayonnaise with lemon juice, and chopped tomatoes.

Roasted Whole Fish with Vegetables

Chinese Noodle Salad with Shrimp

A light, refreshing salad, this tastes especially good in summer, served chilled. It is done in no time at all, as the Chinese noodles don't need to cook long, but simply get doused with boiling water. You can be generous with the spices, as the noodles absorb a lot. The noodles can be purchased in Asian stores, or in the Asian section of a large supermarket.

Serves 4:
2 cloves garlic
1 piece fresh ginger, about 1/2-inch long
4 oz glass (cellophane) noodles
1 bunch fresh Italian parsley
14 oz shrimp, cooked and peeled
Juice of 2 lemons
1 tbs soy sauce
3 tbs vegetable oil
Salt to taste
Freshly ground black pepper to taste

Prep time: about 30 minutes
Per serving: 240 calories
22 g protein/9 g fat
17 g carbohydrates

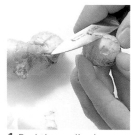

1 Peel the garlic cloves. Peel the ginger, and chop very finely.

2 Pour boiling water over the noodles, and let them soak for about 10 minutes. Then pour them in a strainer, quench with cold water, and cut them into bite-sized pieces with kitchen scissors.

3 Rinse the parsley, shake dry, pick the leaves off the stems, and chop them coarsely. Cut one garlic clove in half lengthwise, and rub the salad bowl with the cut side.

4 Put the shrimp, the Chinese noodles, the parsley, and the ginger into the bowl. Mix the lemon juice with the soy sauce and the oil, add salt and pepper, and add the remaining garlic clove. Pour the dressing over the salad, and mix well. Chill until ready to serve.

Gambas al Ajillo (Garlic Shrimp)

In Spain, the shrimp are eaten as tapas (little bites) with a glass of dry sherry. You can serve them as a little snack or hors d'oeuvre. For a light main course, serve them with rice, and a salad.

Serves 4:
6 cloves garlic
1 small dried chile pepper
1/2 cup olive oil
12 oz shrimp, cooked and peeled
Salt to taste

Prep time: about 10 minutes
Per serving: 190 calories
15 g protein/14 g fat
2 g carbohydrates

2 Heat the olive oil in a pan, and add the garlic and the chile pepper. Stirring constantly, sauté them over low heat until the garlic is golden brown.

4 Season the garlic shrimp with salt, and serve with a fresh baguette as an hors d'oeuvre, or a small supper.

1 Peel the garlic cloves, and slice them finely crossways. Gently press the chile pepper with the side of a knife blade.

3 Stir in the shrimp, and heat them for 2 minutes, continuing to stir.

Credits

Published originally under the title Garlic: Mit Knoblauch, ©1990 Gräfe und Unzer Verlag GmbH, Munich
English translation for the U.S. edition
©2001, Silverback Books, Inc.

Project Editor: Lisa M. Tooker
Editors: Jennifer Newens, CCP, Vené Franco
Translator: Gerda Dinwiddie
Design and Production: Shanti Nelson
Design: Heinz Kraxenberger, Ludwig Kaiser and Robert Gigler
Photos: Odette Teubner and Kerstin Mosney; Erika Casparek-Türkkan (p 5)

Printed in Hong Kong through Global Interprint, Santa Rosa, California.
ISBN: 1-930603-11-8

Cornelea Adam
As a small child, she learned to make herself useful in her parent's hotel in the wine cellar and kitchen: A formal training as hotel manager was logical. Later she was able to utilize her various job related experiences in foreign countries in the trial kitchen as food stylist and as editor of a well-known German women's magazine, translating them into words and pictures. She has been working for three years as an independent food journalist and cookbook author.

Odette Teubner
Teubner was also trained by her father, the internationally known food photographer Christian Teubner. Following that, she dedicated a few month to fashion photography. Today she works exclusively in the studio for food photographer Teubner.

Kerstin Mosney
Mosney completed a college for photography in the French part of Switzerland. Afterwards, she worked as an assistant with different photographers, among them the food photographer Jürgen Tapprich in Zurich. Since 1985 she works in the Photography Studio Teubner.